Contents

KU-076-967

Featured profiles

Careers at a glance

Lucy Davies

Personal Assistant in an importing company

PERSONAL PROFILE

Career: Personal assistant. 'My role is a bit of a hotchpotch really.'

Interests: Singing, running and yoga. ' I also enjoy listening to Latin American music.'

Latest accomplishment: 'Producing four CDs of original Cuban rhythms together in a package with a booklet. It was a big project and a bit of a headache, but fun to do.'

Why I do what I do: 'Because I enjoy it, and I am interested in Latin American culture.'

I am: 'Organized and determined.'

What I wanted to be when I was at school: 'A teacher. Then I read an article where someone said, "I never liked school, so why did I become a teacher?"'

What a personal assistant does

There are many types of personal assistant, or PA. The role of a PA is to help someone else do their job. Lucy Davies' PA work is tied closely to trade with Latin America.

Many of the products we buy in the shops are made in the UK, but there is also a huge market for imported goods, which come from all over the world. Although the UK is a member of the European Union, and a great deal of trade is done with other member nations, there is still consumer demand for goods from further afield. One area that exports to the UK is Latin America, which encompasses the Spanish- or Portuguese- speaking countries of Mexico and Middle and South America, as well as parts of the West Indies.

Lucy works for Tumi, an organization that imports handicrafts and music from Latin America. Mo Fini set it up in 1978 after he travelled through the continent and returned with a few alpaca jumpers to sell on a market stall. Tumi now has four shops of its own in the UK and wholesales to many other shops and organizations. It also has a separate and thriving music label. Lucy's job involves helping Mo do his job effectively – assisting him with all his work requirements.

Fair trade

Mo and the staff at Tumi believe in fair trade. The people making the crafts depend on the buyers who approach them just as the buyers and their colleagues depend on the craftspeople. By becoming involved in the communities, visiting them regularly and paying a fair rate, Tumi is able to give the craftspeople a better income than they would otherwise have.

'We regularly receive shipments from different Latin American countries,' says Lucy. 'These are organized over there by Mo and local managers who liaise with craftspeople and organize the payment and shipment of the goods.' As with any trading organization, when fashions change, the nature of the goods bought and sold must change too. Lucy explains: 'Ten years ago there was a big market in the UK for ethnic handicrafts. Tumi was operating in a market where hardly anyone else was selling Latin American handicrafts. Since then, such products have become less fashionable, and more importers are trading with Latin America.' Because of this, Tumi makes a big effort to get new products into the shops: 'For example, there used to be a big market in brightly-painted balsa wood parrots. This has decreased, so now we sell unpainted parrots in a set with paints and a brush. These sell to children and the educational market. This way we can continue to support the craftspeople and communities we buy from.'

Tropical!

A recent Tumi import from Latin America is music. The Tumi record label signs Latin American musicians and records their music, or buys the rights from other record companies. In particular demand are the 'tropical' rhythms such as salsa, rumba and merengue. 'It's a big dance craze at the moment,' explains Lucy. Tumi Music also records more traditional sounds such as music using Inca wind instruments, played before the Spanish introduced string instruments. So far, Tumi Music has over 80 albums on its list.

Tumi Music produces an extensive catalogue of CDs from very traditional music through to the latest chart sounds.

All in a day's work

Lucy's days vary enormously. For two months of every year she is usually in Latin America. She spends the time 'mostly visiting craftspeople and maintaining our relationships with them. Unless you have the human contact the system wouldn't work – it's a long-term relationship,' explains Lucy. 'It's not just a business relationship but a social thing as well. Mo is godfather to over 20 children in different countries, and I'm godmother to a few too!'

Lucy and Mo bought a fishing boat from this woman for use in an exhibition in the UK. It was being used on Lake Atitlan in Guatemala.

When she's in the UK she works at the Tumi offices or at home, to fit work around her two young children. 'Things are different depending on whether Mo is here, throwing things at me to do,' she explains. 'When he's not here it slows down a bit, and people work more on their own.' Typical work on a quieter day can range from

Lucy works with her colleague Martin Morales. He is bilingual and is the Tumi (Music) Label manager. He uses his Spanish a great deal, particularly when he's talking to Latin American musicians.

ordering books for sale in the shops and liaising with the publishers of a book she and Mo have written about the crafts of Latin America, to taking telephone calls in English or Spanish, sorting out answers to queries, and much more.

Translating 'Expression'

'There's a new CD from a group called Expression,' explains Lucy. 'They are Peruvian and have written notes on the history and culture behind their music. We want these notes in the CD booklet, but they are written in Spanish.' Lucy works at translating these notes, firstly literally, then later she 'tidies it up', until it sounds right to an English speaker. 'Some of this material started in Quechua, an indigenous language in Peru and parts of Bolivia. The band is based in Cuzco, a city in the heart of the indigenous population in Peru, so a lot of the songs were originally written in Quechua. I don't have to translate from Quechua,' laughs

Lucy, 'it has already been translated into Spanish by the band.'

'Sometimes I might get a call from Ecuador, for example,' continues Lucy. 'Perhaps to be told that some jumper knitters want to charge more than we agreed, or that a craftsperson has broken his leg so can't supply an order. I'll either try to put the caller in contact with Mo or sort it out myself.'

Product information

'At the moment I'm doing some work on product information,' says Lucy. 'We like the people working in the shops to know all about the products they are selling, and about the people who make the crafts, so I'm updating the information we have for sending out to the shops. I sent a fax to El Salvador the other day,' she explains, 'asking for information on a product we knew very little about. I got two pages back in Spanish that I needed to translate.'

The Tumi warehouse is the first stopping-off point for imported goods. They are unpacked, checked and stored until needed.

Lucy also deals with the educational packs that Tumi supplies to schools and other interested organizations, writes and produces the Tumi journal, and helps research and make educational videos about Latin American crafts. 'My role is somewhat confusing,' she confesses. 'Over the summer I was helping Mo with the music project and doing a bit of translation as well as inputting stuff into the computer.'

It's a fact

TUMI
Latin American Crafts

The Spanish spoken in Latin America is different from the language spoken in Spain. Certain words have completely different meanings. Each Latin American country has its own way of speaking and different accents. For many of the indigenous people in Latin America, Spanish is their second language, so they may speak it more slowly and carefully than Spanish people, making it easier for the Western ear to understand.

It's a fact

The word Tumi originates from the ancient Peruvian Moche culture and was the name given to a sacrificial knife. As time passed, its use was transformed from an object of ceremony into a surgical instrument, used particularly by the Incas, and later it became a symbol of the God of Healing.

Activity

The market for imported goods is always changing. Successful traders need to watch this and anticipate new trends. Do you have a flair for this?

You will need
For a trader in UK goods: catalogues for mail order goods that give bulk discounts for large orders. (Some catalogues for small toys and novelties do this.)
For a trader in imported goods: access to the Internet.

Procedure (all traders)
1. Allocate yourself an imaginary budget (the money you will need to set up in business and start trading successfully).
2. Decide what line you will trade in. You might consider running a school tuck shop, supplying your friends with practical joke toys, or opening a shop in your local town selling any type of goods. There are many other possibilities.
3. Research your project carefully. Ask your potential customers what they

like buying and how much they would be prepared to pay. Go into shops and find the best selling lines. If possible, and in a quiet moment, speak to the shop staff about this. Ask them how they think the market will move next.
4. Research your suppliers. Is it better to have one or several? If you are considering importing goods, use the Internet to find sources of foreign goods. Are your languages good enough to cope? Would you be able to order and sort out problems in a foreign language? Are you trading fairly?
5. Consider how much stock you would need to set up in business. Remember that it might take several months for new stock to arrive, especially if you are ordering from overseas. How much would this cost? How much would the lease on your shop cost? Also bear in mind the expense of staff wages, and other overheads such as heating, stationery, etc.
6. Set up your 'virtual trading company'. Ask friends to be customers, to 'buy' goods and present some of the problems you might encounter. Could you set up the same company

abroad? What additional problems might this raise?
7. At the end of a certain trading period, count up your income and outgoings. Are you making a profit? If not, why not? Are there certain issues you hadn't considered beforehand? Was your initial budget anywhere near enough to see you through the first few 'months' of trading?
8. Might you consider setting up a real small business? This is good experience, and looks great on your CV. Make sure you talk to an adult about it first. Remember that businesses can lose money as well as make a profit.

The covers of some of the recent albums from Tumi

How to become a personal assistant

Lucy poses with her partner Mo (second from left), their daughter Nina, a close friend and a group of Bolivian weavers.

'My interest in Latin America was first stirred at school,' says Lucy, 'when a geography teacher told us about coffee production and what happened to coffee that couldn't be sold.' She later gained a degree in comparative American studies, which involved learning Spanish. 'There was a wonderful crash course in Spanish,' she recalls. 'Our teacher, Salvador, made us sing Spanish songs and read Spanish poems – it was great fun.' She then spent a year doing residential voluntary work in the UK. 'Then I thought that it was odd to study all these places and not actually go there,' continues Lucy, 'so I arranged some voluntary work and travel in Brazil.'

On her return to the UK, Lucy wanted to something less emotionally demanding and got a job in a Tumi shop. 'When I got to the shop for the interview I just fell in love with it,' she says. She got the job partly because of her Spanish and interest in Latin America.

'Later I left Tumi, went travelling again, then did a six month Pitman course, because I thought office skills would come in useful. I learnt shorthand, typing and word processing and how to be a nice secretary, which I immediately forgot. I did some temping work to use my new skills to see what offices are like: mostly pretty awful. Then the education person at Tumi left and I took over, and my role developed from there.'

Many people do enjoy conventional office work though the role of 'secretary' is becoming less important. This is because many office workers now use computers so they have less need of secretarial backup, but more need of the help a PA can give.

Is this the career for you?

Personal assistants need keyboard and computer skills, and sometimes shorthand. As well as that, more and more PAs need additional languages. 'You need to be able to put your hand to lots of different things,' explains Lucy. 'You need to be adaptable and flexible, organized and efficient.'

For her particular type of PA work, Lucy also needs an eye for photographs, and to be able to find and talk about the appropriate images. She also needs writing and editing skills. 'For example,' says Lucy, 'Mo takes a lot of photographs – it's a big hobby of his. He wanted to make a book of his black and white photographs so I worked on that project, comparing photographs, working on the text and choosing the right printing firm. I also organized an exhibition of some of his photos, posters and postcards.'

'You need to be able to communicate with people,' says Lucy. 'When you're travelling it's more a verbal than a written skill but working here you need to be able to translate.' You don't necessarily need language qualifications: 'Mo has no qualifications in Spanish,' says Lucy. 'You just need to be happy to use the language.'

Career planning

Visit shops selling imported artefacts. Talk to the shop assistants about the goods, where they came from, who made them and how they got to this country.

Find out about local companies that import or export goods. Ask one of their linguists to speak to your group about the day-to-day work.

Making Career Connections

Ask your careers adviser about courses in office skills. Find out about other qualifications it might be useful to have, especially language qualifications.

Contact a secretarial temping agency to ask about their requirements. Find out about the demand for bilingual personal assistants. Ask how good your languages need to be to enable you to find interesting work.

Getting started

Interested in being a personal assistant? Here's what you can do now.

1. Learn how to use word processing and office management programs on the computer. Use these skills at home or school if you can, and set up a mock office to practise with.

2. Keep studying a broad range of subjects including maths, English and languages.

3. Try to spend some time abroad on an exchange visit. or even better, try to get work abroad in the holidays or gap year. The best way to gain fluency in another language is to speak it all day, every day.

4. Use the Internet to practise your written languages. 'Meet' people in other countries this way and start corresponding.

Related careers

Here are some related carers you may want to look into.

Wholesale assistant

Sells imported products to shops and through catalogues. Attends trade shows, packs orders, sorts out problems, sells on the telephone. May need to contact suppliers so a knowledge of languages can be important.

Label assistant

If working in world music, imports and markets music from other countries. Needs to speak and read languages to deal with the artistes and agree contracts.

Shop assistant

Unpacks, displays and sells imported artefacts. Arranges window displays, cashes up, deals with enquiries, liaises with head office. May attend trade fairs, take stands at concerts, etc. Languages could be useful in any of these situations.

Office manager

Runs the day-to-day workings of an office: orders stationery and furniture, liaises with cleaners, contractors, and others; supports all office staff.

Future watch

There will always be a need for the support work of personal assistants, although as the workplace evolves so the necessary skills change. Languages are definitely a must for many PA roles now. The world market is growing and businesses like Tumi will continue to thrive for as long as they keep track of markets and change accordingly. The world music market is growing especially quickly.

'My role is a bit of a hotchpotch really'

Shahed Ahmad

Community Interpreter

PERSONAL PROFILE

Career: Community interpreter. 'I interpret exactly what is said, without adding or missing anything.'

Interests: Sport and fitness, socializing, parties, music, computing, helping out in the community.

Latest accomplishment: 'I did a course on community counselling which links in with my interpreting work.'

Why I do what I do: 'There's a large Bengali community in my town and not many people have access to services because of the language gap. Some unqualified people work as interpreters and sometimes things go wrong – so I thought it would be a good thing to do.'

I am: 'Friendly and helpful, patient and calm. I always keep people's confidences.'

What I wanted to be when I was at school: 'A pilot, but I went to live in Bangladesh for part of my schooling and there weren't many courses relating to flying.'

What a community interpreter does

Cities and towns have many communities within them, and some of these communities are based on a common religion, country of origin or language. Although younger members of these communities find it easy to integrate into the prevailing culture, older people often find it hard to learn a new language and new customs. This is generally not a problem, but in certain situations, having English as only their second language can be worrying or even dangerous. Community interpreters help to bridge that language and cultural gap by providing a sympathetic interpreting service to people who need to communicate with medical, social services or housing staff, or perhaps have to appear in a court of law.

Shahed Ahmad is a community interpreter working within the Bengali-speaking community in his home town. 'My ambition has always been to help out the community,' Shahed says. When he heard about a course to become a community interpreter he jumped at the chance. There are many occasions when interpreters are needed: 'Most of the work is in hospitals,' explains Shahed. 'People become afraid when they can't understand or speak the language. They may get the wrong information. Most people tend to take their young children along to interpret for them at a GP's surgery but the hospital is more serious and they really need to know what is going on.' Shahed has also helped many people needing to understand the benefits system at social security offices.

Community links

Community interpreters don't necessarily need to be a part of the community where they work – in fact, it can help if they're not. Because of the private nature of

Shahed's ambition has always been to do some type of community work. By using his bilingual skills, he can really help the Bengali people in his home town.

In some communities clients may also be relations or friends, although the project manager will ensure this doesn't happen unless the client is happy about it.

many of the meetings Shahed attends, it is best if he doesn't know his clients. 'The administrator of the local Interpreting Project calls to ask whether I know a client,' says Shahed. 'The administrator also needs to match up the person's sex and age with the interpreter's. There can be many religious and cultural aspects. An older generation woman wouldn't want a younger person to interpret for her as she may be embarrassed.'

All in a day's work

Today Shahed is interpreting for a client who is going to appear in court. He has been asked to meet the man at the court building half an hour before his case comes up. 'I was called in by the man's English-speaking solicitor, who knew the court appearance would be a problem for him,' explains Shahed. 'This meeting is called a pre-session. The solicitor talks to the client through me. The client did not know what the results of the court case could be, so was quite afraid.' The solicitor explains everything and Shahed interprets as precisely as he can. 'I also explain to the client not to say anything he doesn't want me to translate, as I will interpret exactly what he says.'

Shahed shows a client his identity card. Many clients are wary of interpreters as some have been known to breach their clients' confidentiality. The identity card shows that Shahed is a trained interpreter and that he can be trusted.

explains Shahed, 'as I hadn't been to a court before and thought the client might blame me if he was found guilty,' he laughs. 'But once I did one of these cases the next was more relaxed.'

There are some things that

Shahed talks with a client before meeting the service provider. This may be to help him understand complex matters or simply to relax with and get to know the client.

In open court

'When we go into the courtroom I am given the Koran to swear on. I explain my role to the court, especially that I am impartial, that I will keep the client's confidentiality and interpret everything that is said. I also ask them to speak in short sentences and pause as often as possible, otherwise I might miss something. At first I was quite nervous,'

Shahed will not interpret. 'If somebody in court made a racial comment that might offend my client and does not relate to the matter, then I would ask them to put it in a nicer way,' he says.

Confidentiality

Keeping secrets can be difficult in close-knit communities, and some clients have used interpreters who went on to discuss their private

matters with other people. This is strictly forbidden and Shahed and his trained and experienced colleagues would only do it in the most extreme circumstances. 'If it's a matter of life and death then I could break a confidence. This might be in a case of domestic violence or child abuse. I would talk to the Interpreting Project about this.' The Project has guidelines for summoning help from Social Services.

Too much lunch...

Shahed relates another of his recent cases: 'A chap in his 60s, who was quite overweight and who had already been to hospital with heart problems, went to see a hospital dietician. I was interpreting for him. I had already been given information about the appointment so I could check some hospital vocabulary beforehand.' This is an important part of Shahed's work, as some sessions can include detailed technical information. He makes his own glossaries (list of words) to help in these situations. 'The dietician was asking about his diet and daily food intake. I know the diet of Bengali people and so I asked him: "Didn't you have any fish curry for lunch?" 'laughs Shahed. 'The man admitted that he had.' This was all done in a friendly and helpful manner. 'A lot of funny things happen,' says Shahed, 'Often the service provider and client are laughing while I interpret.'

Freelance work

Shahed works as a freelance, which means that whenever there is work available and the Project calls to offer it, he can choose whether to take it or not. He is then paid for the amount of work he does. Some weeks he is very busy and other weeks less so. Shahed and many other freelances supplement their interpreting work with other work.

The interpreting contract

The Interpreting Project that trained and pays Shahed is funded by joint finance monies from local health authorities. They want to ensure that their clients are able to use their services whether English is their first language or not. Other organizations use the service but have to pay for it as they use it, except local voluntary organizations who use the service free of charge. The service providers, such as the health service, the benefits offices, the courts and so on, pay for the interpreting service either through their initial funding or as they use the service. Shahed's clients do not pay.

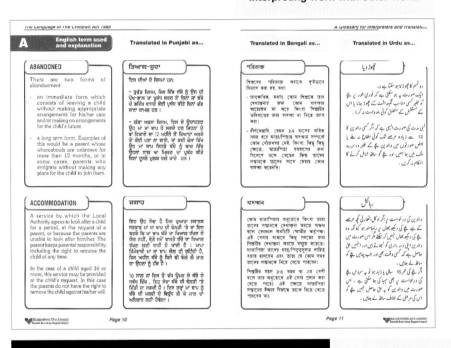

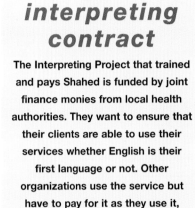

This is part of a glossary to help interpreters who have to use the terms from the Children Act of 1989. It provides translation into Bengali, Punjabi and Urdu.

Activity

Emergency!
Imagine you are interpreting for a client who is attending a hospital appointment. Decide on a medical problem (a heart problem perhaps) and the type of doctor your client will be seeing. Decide, too, which additional language is being spoken and how much English the client understands and speaks.

Procedure
1. Make a glossary of the vocabulary you are likely to need.
2. Think about the way the appointment may proceed. Are you ready to advise your client that the doctor wishes to examine him or her? Have you considered possible problems with this, especially if the doctor and client are not the same sex? And where will you be at this stage?
3. With two friends, role-play the pre-session, where you meet to reassure your client beforehand, and then the appointment itself. Take turns playing the different roles. If you are not yet fluent enough in your second language you may use English where necessary.
4. Imagine there is a problem: the wait for the doctor is too long; the client misunderstands what the doctor wants, or the client is taken suddenly ill. What additional problems does this create? How do you cope with them?
5. Is the client reassured by your interpreting service? Are you friendly and helpful and clearly on the client's 'side'? How could you perform better?

How to become a community interpreter

Shahed saw the Project advertising for bilingual people to learn to become community interpreters, and signed up for the eight-week part-time course. 'It was more like a social gathering,' recalls Shahed. 'We did role-plays, acting out a client, a service provider and an interpreter. This gave us a general idea of what it is like to be all three. We also talked about confidentiality and impartiality and about people's cultural and religious backgrounds. We swore an oath about confidentiality and that we would build trust with our clients so that they can talk freely.'

Shahed continues 'At the end of the course we submitted a glossary of 200 items, 20 on each area such as housing, health, social services, etc.' This glossary was more how Shahed would explain an item to somebody, rather than simply the word from the dictionary. He also researched 50 useful community contact names and addresses that his clients might find useful. Otherwise the course was geared up to the spoken, not written, language: 'The course is not related to translation and a lot of people don't have a formal knowledge of their language,' explains Shahed. At the end of the course he received a certificate and an identity card.

Shahed has also learnt the basics of community counselling. The director of his mosque does some counselling and this interests Shahed: 'I did a course about understanding people's problems, listening skills, and about how counselling is a chance for people to talk to somebody to relieve their anxieties. I want to do more of this because it relates to interpreting work; maybe I will link them together and go into social work. I don't just do it for the sake of work. I understand these people's cultural background and have the same religion. I do understand their problems.'

This interpreter (the woman in the centre) speaks three languages. She is helping a client (right) with a medical problem that is being diagnosed by a doctor (left). She has a glossary of relevant words and phrases to hand.

Is this the career for you?

Anyone who speaks more than one language can work as an interpreter but as Shahed explains, there is more to it than that: 'You need a good speaking ability of two languages,' he explains. 'And you also need self-discipline, as you need to be on time for sessions. You need to be both assertive and polite and have an understanding of cultural and religious differences.' An understanding of racial problems is also important. Confidentiality is one of the most important aspects of the service: 'You have to be able to keep confidences and be non-judgmental.'

Community interpreters do not need a great written ability with their languages. Research skills and common-sense, however, are useful when planning a session and when things don't go as expected. You also need to dress appropriately: 'In court I wear a jacket and tie,' says Shahed. He dresses to suit the particular situation. And what does he think of his new career? 'I enjoy doing this work,' says Shahed.

Career planning

Contact your local council or social services to find out about community interpreting projects running in your area.

Ask your careers advisor about careers in social work. Find out about courses and qualifications. Ask how many opportunities there are for people with two or more languages.

Making Career Connections

Ask an administrator or tutor and an interpreter to come and speak to your group about the work of the project or service.

Visit your careers service and find out about these and other courses leading to qualifications in interpreting. Ask about other types of interpreting work.

Getting started

Interested in being a community interpreter? Here's what you can do now.

1. Keep studying all your languages. Make sure that you are fluent. Consider an exchange trip to increase your verbal abilities.
2. Read newspapers and magazines in your additional languages. Keep them up-to-date this way. Work on your written languages too.
3. Do your own research into local community groups and what each does for the community. Consider joining any that you are interested in. Talk to people about language problems within the groups and think how these could be resolved.
4. Do your own bit of 'freelance' work – ask whether people you know might consider hiring you for an hour to help out in some way. Think about how people might tie freelance work in with other jobs or commitments.

Related careers

Here are some related careers you may want to look into.

Esol (English for Speakers of Other Languages) teacher

Teaches English to people whose first language is not English. Teaching may take place in community centres, colleges, or in the home.

Social worker

Deals in many aspects of community work, including work within immigrant communities to help people integrate.

Community counsellor

Works within a community as a listening ear for people's problems. Helps people think their own problems through in a secure non-judgemental environment.

Youth worker

Works with young people within the community, in clubs, drop-in centres or on the street. Befriends and helps young people with problems.

Future watch

There will always be a wide range of work within the community, and interpreters will be needed as long as there are language barriers. Since the European Community has relaxed its migration rules there are increasing numbers of non-native speaking communities that need support from within and from Social Services and other government-funded projects.

Shahed (far right) with the other trainee interpreters on the course. The Interpreting Project, which trained and employs Shahed, can provide interpreters in 26 different languages.

Karen Henderson

Cabin Assistant

PERSONAL PROFILE

Career: Cabin assistant. 'I serve passengers on board a boat.'

Interests: 'Swimming, cinema, socializing, music, eating out and making clothes. I go to France regularly to see friends.'

Latest accomplishment: 'I've been acting as senior cabin assistant because she is absent at the moment.'

Why I do what I do: 'I enjoy meeting people, using my French and travelling. I like the atmosphere of working in the travel industry.'

I am: 'Determined, level-headed, stubborn, logical thinking and calm under pressure.'

What I wanted to be when I was at school: 'I had no idea at all.'

What a cabin assistant does

Millions of people make journeys by boat and ship every year. As ferries often travel between countries, the passengers on any one vessel may speak a variety of languages. All of these people and their needs have to be catered for on board.

Karen Henderson works as one of a team of cabin crew aboard a fast ferry called the *Stena Lynx 111* which runs between Newhaven in the UK and Dieppe in France. The boat is a catamaran: 'It goes at high speeds because it has four engines and two hulls, which are very light and raised out of the water,' says Karen. The majority of passengers are British, yet there are also many French people using the service. Karen is English-speaking and also fluent in French so in her job as cabin assistant she can help passengers from either side of the English Channel.

'I work in various areas,' says Karen, 'the café, the bar, the information desk or the shop, to make sure passengers are satisfied, provide them with a service and make their journey as comfortable as possible.' The staff on board work together in various teams. 'There's the master (or captain), the first officer, and chief and assistant engineer. Also the general purpose operatives (the people on the car deck who load the cars), plus the people working in my area.'

Safety first

The number of staff working with Karen as cabin crew varies depending on the number of passengers. 'We've got the cabin manager, the senior cabin assistant and then a minimum of ten cabin assistants. If there's an emergency we need a certain number of people to direct the passengers. If we didn't have enough crew then we would have to turn away passengers,' Karen explains.

Karen sometimes works in the information office during the crossing. She uses her French more here than on other duties.

The *Stena Lynx 111*, the catamaran that Karen works aboard, was built in Australia in 1996. It has the capacity to carry 627 passengers and 36 crew.

Karen works a rota system of 12-hour days, four days working a certain shift then the next four days off. There are two shifts, the day shift and the night shift. If she is working the day shift she makes two return journeys to France. On the night shift there is only one return journey followed by other duties while the boat remains in port between midnight and 6am.

Karen is working the day shift and her alarm goes very early: 'I get up at a quarter to five. I don't enjoy getting up early but I can do it – I've never overslept. Then I dress in my Star Trek uniform!' she jokes. She has a strict dress code and has to make sure she is well groomed, with her hair drawn back correctly and minimal jewellery.

Once she is dressed she drives to the port and meets the other cabin crew in the briefing room. 'The cabin manager checks that there's enough crew and briefs us on what kind of passengers we've got, and anything different that's going to happen that day. She tells us where we will be working, and when she's

Staff on the car deck direct drivers. They must wear high-visibility coats at all times in this area.

satisfied that we've got enough crew we walk down through the port in our high visibility coats.' The cabin crew reach the boat just before the passengers: 'The boat's been made ready by the night crew,' Karen explains.

As soon as she is on board, Karen, who is working as senior cabin assistant for the day, starts to prepare a muster list by inserting a disk into the computer. 'It's a list of everyone on board, from the master and first officer down. The list is radioed ashore, faxed all over the place and goes to the bridge before we can sail.' This is a safety precaution so that it is always known exactly who is on board the boat.

Safety first and safety second...

'I give a muster card to each member of our department. We have to memorize this, and there are strict drills and checks all the time. A muster card might say: At Incident XYZ do such-and-such a thing, such as clear the toilets of passengers. Then if an announcement "Incident XYZ" came over the tannoy we'd all know exactly what to do.'

Near departure time, the deck supervisor, who is loading cars on the car deck, radios up and says: 'Cabin manager, passengers boarding'. This is the cabin crew's cue to go to their embarkation positions. 'We stand at each doorway,' says Karen, 'with our uniforms buttoned up and hats on and greet the passengers as they come up.'

Karen distributes the muster cards she has prepared to all the crew on board.

Making a difference

If the boat is due to be full, it can be a hectic time as the passengers board: 'I find seats for the passengers, direct them to the Club Class lounge and tell them where the toilets or information desk are.' This is when Karen starts using her French, and any of her conversations with passengers from now on could be in either language. The passengers need to feel at home, and Karen's team is there to reassure and help.

The next task is to make a passenger announcement. A colleague usually makes the English announcement but Karen always does the one in French: 'I welcome the passengers aboard, tell them the expected sailing time and that the shop and café will be opening shortly,' says Karen. After the safety video is played the boat leaves port and Karen's duties

Karen and her colleagues prepare the shop for the day's customers.

switch to the duty free shop. 'I finish stocking up with newspapers. By the time we're ready to open there are always passengers queuing outside!'

Retail duties

Karen is the retail leader and oversees everything that happens in the shop. This includes supervising up to six staff, stocking up, re-ordering goods and answering customer queries. 'They'll ask my advice about perfume, what promotions we've got on, or how much duty-free shopping they can take into the country.' These questions can be in English or French so Karen changes between the two languages all day. 'They ask other questions as well, such as where the railway station can be found on shore, things like that. The customer contact is very satisfying.'

The shop closes 15 minutes before reaching the French port. Karen stocks up, makes another passenger announcement in French and generally cleans and tidies up. There isn't much time to get everything ready for the return trip: 'We're only in port for 40 minutes, sometimes less, it was 20 minutes yesterday as we were trying to catch up time!' laughs Karen. Then the next set of passengers starts boarding. 'This crossing is quieter and carries mostly French people. This is better. When I learnt my language I wanted to use it, and if I'm talking to passengers they're generally French on this crossing.'

Did you know?

Normal ferries have large life rafts that lower down on a crane but fast ferries have MES (Marine Evacuation System) chutes. These are large inflatable containers that are packed with a life raft and form slides for passengers to descend before landing in the inflatable life raft at the bottom. All cabin crew are trained to inflate the MES ready for use.

The *Stena Lynx 111* is due back in the UK port at midday, although it can be delayed due to bad weather conditions. But this isn't the end of Karen's day. There is a longer wait at port this time to get stores on board, then the crew take the boat for a second return crossing, and this can be delayed too: 'We got in at 10pm last night. If it's this late I drive home, go straight to bed, get five hours sleep then start all over again! You've just got to accept it really. But then I get four days off, the nights aren't nearly as hectic, and I sometimes get home early to compensate for extra hours on the day shift.'

Activity

Cross-Channel ferries have an impressive recent safety record – largely due to the procedures and regulations in place to safeguard passengers. Imagine you are planning the safety procedures for the cabin crew on a boat like the *Stena Lynx 111*. You need to decide, in advance, what the 12 cabin staff would need to do in the event of a minor emergency in port which leads to the boat being evacuated. Ask some friends to become 'crew' and number your staff before you start.

Draw a plan of the boat (you can invent a boat layout and staffing details) and make a chart to help planning. Here are some questions you need to ask yourself:

1. How many staff do you have? What are their safety qualifications (first aid at sea, qualified to drive a lifeboat, and so on)?
2. How many different languages do the passengers and staff speak? Will instructions be understood?
3. How many areas of the boat might passengers need to be evacuated from? How do you ensure that no passengers are left on board?
4. Think how you might word the announcement to ask passengers to disembark? If people start to panic it could make this minor incident into a major problem – how do you avoid this? Can you translate this announcement into another language to address all the passengers?
5. Create 'muster cards' the size of credit cards for yourself and eleven staff. What three main instructions will be on each card? The cards will need to be different for the various members of staff.
6. If you have enough people, enact the emergency situation.
7. Try the whole procedure in a different language.

How to become a cabin assistant

Karen has been interested in the French language from an early age: 'I did a summer exchange with a French girl for five years,' she explains. Karen went on to read French and history at university and emerged knowing that she wanted to use her language in her work. 'I worked for a campsite tour operator for one season, then applied for a temporary position in personnel.' She helped deal with the company's French employees, and did some translation work, some of it technical: 'Items such as memos from the port manager in the UK to the port manager in France – using words I didn't even understand in English!' It was here that Karen heard about the new Stena boat, and the company started advertising for staff. Her boss encouraged her to apply, and months later she was jumping off platforms into cold swimming pools. Her basic training had begun!

Karen sells tickets to the first class lounge from the information desk.

Moving up

'I want to work the information desk as I'd use my French more. I'm career-oriented, I've got to go somewhere and I thrive on personal responsibility. If I become the senior cabin assistant I'll stay in the job.' There are only limited openings, though, so Karen is also looking at the possibility of working in France or moving within the UK travel industry. 'I'd have to use my French,' she says. But of her current role she says: 'The experience you get from it is good. If someone wants enjoyment in using their languages they'll get it in this job.'

Is this the career for you?

However tired and irritated they may feel at times, it is part of a cabin assistant's job to be patient and courteous towards the passengers.

'The job may sound tedious,' says Karen, 'as what I do every day is basically the same, but it's the contact I have with the customers that makes it interesting.' It can be frustrating at times: 'If the boat is late and a customer complains it's easy to want to say: "Do you think I want to be here either? I want to go home as much as you do."' However, Karen has the ability to stay cool and courteous and explain the complaints procedure to passengers.

'I like working in a team,' she says, explaining that this is an important part of the work. Also, if the boat is pulled off the route, as it was last winter, staff must be flexible enough to work from another port.

Karen even ended up sleeping one week out of two on a regular ferry to comply with the muster list requirements. You need confidence in your second language and in your ability to deal with passengers and crew. And what about sea legs? 'As a rule, even if it's rough I don't get sick – though I can feel very shaky and green.'

Karen continues, 'It's a young person's atmosphere. Everyone sticks together. It's fun. I really enjoy the job.

'It's a young person's atmosphere. Everyone sticks together. It's fun. I really enjoy the job'

Career planning

Visit a port and if possible, take a ferry crossing. Watch and listen to the cabin assistants at work. Ask them about their job.

Making Career Connections

Arrange to work-shadow someone whose job involves customer care. Is this the sort of work you would like to do?

Organize a day trip on a ferry through your school or club. Note how the ferry company operates its booking and other systems. If it is an international crossing ask how many of the staff are multi-lingual.

Ask your careers advisor about degree courses in languages and business. Do any of them include a travel or tourism option?

Getting started

Interested in being a cabin assistant? Here's what you can do now.

1. Take a serious interest in your language studies. Consider the number of careers open to people with fluency in one or more foreign languages.
2. Take part in your school's foreign exchange programme, a number of times if possible.
3. Listen to foreign radio and read foreign books and magazines to get a feel for the living language.
4. See if you can organize a work placement abroad, even if only for a few weeks.
5. After leaving school, consider spending a year abroad.
6. Join or start a languages club or a cultural society at your school. Look at the way people abroad speak and live.
7. Get a holiday job in the hospitality business. Try waiting at table, working at a leisure centre: anything that involves customer contact.
8. Write to ferry companies to ask about openings that require languages. Find out which languages are most in demand.

Related careers

Here are some related careers you may want to look into.

Air cabin crew member
Provides a similar service but on aeroplanes.

Campsite courier
Looks after families holidaying abroad, often helping with children's clubs. Positions may later arise in area management or head office.

Passenger service agent
Works in ship or airline travel offices or airports, selling tickets and checking passengers in.

Car rental agent
Works in offices around the world as well as at head office, often based in major tourist centres and airports.

Cruise ship worker
Performs any of hundreds of tasks aboard a cruise liner.

Future watch

Cross-Channel ferry companies are under stiff competition from the Channel Tunnel, but they are holding their own and provide a good training ground for work in management or related areas. The experience gained using languages in this environment will always be useful in a variety of other areas in the tourism and hospitality industries.

There is a large variety of jobs aboard a passenger ferry. These people work in the small kitchen area of *Stena Lynx 111*.

Fayçal Chaabane

Telephone representative

PERSONAL PROFILE

Career: Telephone representative. 'I represent my employer on the telephone.'

Interests: 'Fishing – off the pier sometimes. I play football and swim. I like computers.'

Latest accomplishment: 'I was appointed to a more senior position last year. I accomplish lots of things every day as a part of my daily tasks.'

Why I do what I do: 'I like helping people with their difficulties when they are abroad, and helping them sort out their problems. I like making people happy.'

I am: 'Normal! Helpful, diplomatic, honest.'

What I wanted to be when I was at school: A pilot. 'I like flying and flying machines.'

What a telephone representative does

Every organization uses the telephone as one of many ways of communicating. A telephone representative is the person who 'connects' outsiders with the organization, either by calling people or by receiving calls when people ring in. The telephone call can be on any topic – it could be a sales call or a courtesy call, or it could be a customer calling in for help. This last type is the sort of call Fayçal Chaabane receives. He works as a telephone representative for American Express (Amex), a financial services company. Amex sells travellers cheques in many different currencies. These are a safe way of carrying money abroad because it is easy to replace them if they are lost or stolen. When they do go missing, it is Fayçal that people contact.

Fayçal wears a headset which leaves his hands free to reach for a file or look up information in a directory while he is speaking.

'When people buy travellers cheques,' explains Fayçal, 'they get a whole pack with lots of information written in it. This is basically a contract that they sign, which explains what to do if the cheques are lost or stolen. They also get a little card with telephone numbers on. These are freephone numbers to call from anywhere in the world. Hotels and banks also have this number so that travellers can find it easily at any time.'

World-wide centres

There are three Amex travellers cheque centres – one in the UK, one in Salt Lake City in the USA and one in Sydney, Australia. These service different parts of the

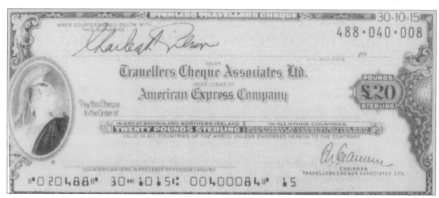

world but when one is closed (because it is night time in that country) the calls are automatically put through to another centre. 'I can get a call from anywhere in the world,' says Fayçal. As well as helping distressed customers, Fayçal may get a call from a bank asking him whether it is all right to cash a customer's cheques. 'We have computer encashment,' explains Fayçal, 'But not every bank or hotel is linked to this. I ask them a couple of questions: Are they happy with the presenter? Have the bank staff watched the signature being written and compared it with the original? If we are both

happy I release an authorization code and the bank staff cash the cheque.'

Fayçal also helps Amex clients in other ways if he can. 'People call to say they have lost their passports or airline tickets,' he reports. 'We advise them by telling them how to fly home without their passports and so on.' Fayçal has a file of thank you letters from customers who had problems which he solved. 'I enjoy doing it,' he says. 'I enjoy helping people.'

Chasing lost luggage

Fayçal won an Amex 'Great Performer' award for helping an elderly couple recover important luggage that had gone astray. The couple were travelling to Italy to a holiday and family reunion when their luggage went astray. This contained vital medication as well as the husband's valued war photographs. Although it was not strictly Fayçal's responsibility, he spent five days tracking down their luggage after the coach company failed to do so. The cases were heading for Somalia and Fayçal arranged for them to be sent to an Italian airport, then collected by taxi and delivered to the couple, all at Amex's expense. 'I was very angry about their treatment,' says Fayçal, 'and I just wanted to sort things out for them.'

All in a day's work

Fayçal works from a desk in an open-plan office, but often it feels to him as though he is somewhere entirely different. 'I take about 300 calls a day on busy days,' he says.

'I put myself into other people's shoes and feel what they feel. I get emotionally involved even though I don't know them and can't see them. I basically travel with them to wherever they are. I know I'm in the UK but at the same time I hear the cicadas in the background and the sound takes me there.'

Fayçal takes calls via the computer on his desk. 'It could be in any language. I can see where the call is coming from but that doesn't mean I know what language the customer will be speaking.' Fayçal will try to converse with the caller in English, French, German, Italian or Arabic, his five main languages. 'I attempt to find a common language,' Fayçal explains. 'Usually I will speak in English first and say "do you speak English?". As they are travellers they usually have enough English, or another common language, to say no and explain what language they do speak.'

Leaping hurdles

Although he can get by in most European languages, there are some that Fayçal knows he cannot converse in. Russian is one of these. 'I know what language they are speaking - it's part of being experienced in this work. If it's Russian I transfer it to a colleague, call one of our offices in Russia and ask them to translate, or call a

It is all too easy to drop your documents or travellers cheques while enjoying yourself on holiday.

Sometimes a colleague asks Fayçal for advice, or may be able to help him. There are many telephone representatives working alongside Fayçal in this worldwide operation.

language bank which finds a translator.' The translator joins in the conversation with Fayçal and the customer.

Once this first hurdle has been overcome and Fayçal and his client are communicating, the problem emerges. Most calls are from banks which need authorization before cashing travellers cheques, and which don't have the right computer to check this on-line; or from clients who are in difficulties. 'Clients are often upset,' says Fayçal. 'They may have lost a lot of money through theft or con deals, or just mislaid it. First I ask for their name and try to find out more information, such as the cause of the problem and what's going on. If the travellers cheques have been stolen I need the numbers. I need these as soon as possible to put them in our computer system.' Fayçal may have to find these numbers from the place of purchase if the client does not have them. 'The computer creates a file so that anyone who tries to cash the cheques anywhere in the world will create a "hit". If this is a thief in a bank somewhere, the staff confiscate the cheques and have the thief arrested.'

Diplomacy

'We do all this in a diplomatic way,' continues Fayçal. 'We don't bombard the client with too many questions.' As well as carefully making enquiries, Fayçal speaks with bank staff and verifies details as a double-check. 'After taking all this information, I evaluate the claim and if I'm entirely happy I will reimburse the client straight away.' Fayçal taps this information into the computer or speaks to bank staff, and the client has the money within five minutes of finishing the call. 'It probably took me six months to build it up, but now I have the experience to know if the claim is genuine,' explains Fayçal.

Instant translation

Fayçal listens and speaks in the customer's language but the computer only understands English. He must translate all the relevant information in his head as he goes along, and tap in the relevant facts in English. 'This is difficult,' he says, 'especially with Arabic names. They can be written in hundreds of ways.' It is important to get the spelling exactly right or the computer will not recognize the customer. 'I have to ask exactly how it is written in their passport,' Fayçal explains.

Fayçal works in a busy open-plan office. But when he takes a call from a distressed client, he focuses entirely on them, ignoring the distractions all around him.

Activity

Spot the language
Can you tell one foreign language from another? Why not try?

Procedure:
With a group of friends, each write the names of three languages on pieces of paper. Fold the pieces of paper, put them in a hat and each take three. Go to the reference library and find guide books to countries where these languages are spoken. Then look at the section in each that gives useful travellers' phrases, along with pronunciation tips. Copy down three phrases in each language and practise speaking them.

Back in your group, take it in turns to speak one phrase in one of 'your' languages and see if the others know which language it is. How can they tell? Is it very like English, or very different? Is it perhaps similar to another foreign language? By the time you have read your third phrase in a certain language, are the others starting to recognize it? Or does it take longer than this to get a 'feel' for a language?

Can you tell what the phrases mean? Are some people in the group better at recognizing the languages, or some better at speaking them? Does this mean they'd be good linguists?

How to become a telephone representative

Telephone work requires all sorts of skills, and with the widening of the global economy, more and more commercial careers of all types require languages. The primary skill needed for Fayçal's job is to be multilingual. Fayçal was brought up speaking two languages, French and Arabic. 'This was good in a way,' he explains, 'but difficult in other ways.' At school, for instance, he had to prepare all his subjects in two languages - twice as much work! At school he also 'picked up' Italian and English.

There is a certain amount of administration involved in most jobs. Sometimes Fayçal needs to copy documents, carry out a customer survey from his calls, or compensate hotels and banks that have reimbursed clients on Amex' behalf.

After leaving school, Fayçal went to Germany and studied the language for a year before working as a translator for an embassy. 'I used to take delegations to places in Germany and interpret for them. I enjoyed the job itself, especially travelling with such friendly people.' He spent seven years in Germany, part of it with a commercial company. 'I did administration, some translation from Arabic and French into German, and vice versa. Then they sent me to work in Tunisia, which involved the same sort of thing, only more of it! It was very hard work, especially as I wasn't used to the Tunisian work culture. I introduced new European management ideas, particularly better treatment of the staff. They couldn't believe it, but it encouraged the workers.' Fayçal left Tunisia to work with Amex. 'We tend to get people coming from universities now,' he says, 'with manpower from all over the world.'

Is this the career for you?

'You need to be a very helpful person, and obviously your languages need to be there. Everybody here has a sense of humour – you need this, and patience to a certain degree.' Fayçal talks of a rapport building automatically with customers. "As soon as you pick up the 'phone you know what sort of person it is straight away. If they're serious so am I, if they chat and joke I chat and joke with them – it's just diplomacy on the telephone.

'I work shifts,' says Fayçal. 'From seven in the morning until three, or two until nine in the evening. The centre used to be open 24 hours a day but it no longer is.' This is because calls are transferred to one of the other centres at night. 'I work weekends too sometimes.'

'You need to be willing to learn. We have skills training, on how to use the computers, to learn the procedures we follow.'

Fayçal gives this final piece of advice: 'If you want to be a linguist it is best to go abroad to master the language and how it is spoken within that country. What you learn at school and university are the basic reading and writing skills, but not spoken skills. Go and work abroad for at least a year.'

Fayçal won a special award for the great lengths he went to to track down the lost luggage of an elderly couple. 'I enjoy helping people' he says.

Career planning

See if you can visit a company that has a number of telephone representatives. You might find telephone salespeople in all sorts of organizations. Try newspapers and other publishers as well as manufacturers and companies like Amex.

Making Career Connections

See if you can find part-time telephone work, perhaps voluntary work for a charity, and ask the people there what it is they enjoy about it.

Talk to your careers adviser about telephone work with languages. Ask which other types of organizations presently rely heavily on linguists, and which might in the future.

Find out about degree courses in more than one language. Send for university prospectuses. Where would you spend the sandwich year? Consider a gap year abroad to ensure your spoken languages are excellent.

Getting started

Interested in becoming a telephone representative? Here's what you can do now.

1. Keep studying as many languages as you can.
2. Practise your communications skills whenever you can: at a debating society, discussing issues with friends, writing letters to the local paper, and so on.
3. Think about how you use the telephone, and practise your 'phone skills. Learn to empathize with the person who calls you.
4. Find a part-time job using the telephone. If you cannot find paid work, look for a commission-only sales role or voluntary work – you may not end up richer but you'll gain a lot from the experience.

Related careers

Here are some related careers you may want to look into.

Telephone salesperson
Contacts buyers by telephone and offers items or services for sale. May also visit clients.

Customer services
Provides the first contact for an organization's customers who have queries, recommendations or complaints. Hands these queries on to other staff or follows them through.

Translator
Provides instant translation services for organizations needing to speak to foreigners. Also does written translations, often working freelance.

Administrator
Handles any type of administration within an organization, including the translation of telephone calls and other communications in foreign languages.

Future watch

Financial services form an important and growing sector of our economy, and despite any changes brought about by the introduction of a common European currency, financial services will continue to be necessary at home and throughout the world.

'As long as there is a language barrier there will always be jobs for people with languages,' says Fayçal. 'This is especially so with European and Far Eastern languages. Language skills will always be needed.'

Suzanne Mantell

Tourist Information Officer

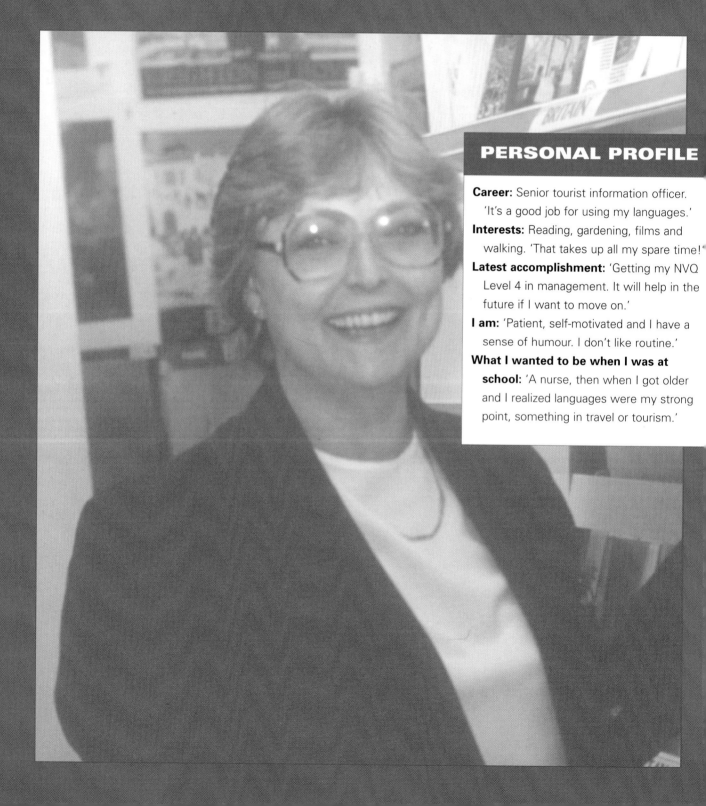

PERSONAL PROFILE

Career: Senior tourist information officer. 'It's a good job for using my languages.'

Interests: Reading, gardening, films and walking. 'That takes up all my spare time!'

Latest accomplishment: 'Getting my NVQ Level 4 in management. It will help in the future if I want to move on.'

I am: 'Patient, self-motivated and I have a sense of humour. I don't like routine.'

What I wanted to be when I was at school: 'A nurse, then when I got older and I realized languages were my strong point, something in travel or tourism.'

What a tourist information officer does

In every town and city there are tourist information centres (TICs) to help people with any queries they may have about that town. The tourist information officers (TIOs) who work in them answer enquiries on a wide range of topics. These range from finding accommodation, discovering local attractions and events, booking coach tickets and helping with

but a significant proportion are from foreign visitors who speak little or no English. 'Everyone who works in this TIC has to speak at least one foreign European language,' explains Suzanne. 'We cover French, German, Spanish and Italian. In the summer a good third of my day will be spent dealing with foreign visitors.'

Suzanne also answers telephone

Languages

'French is the most used language here,' explains Suzanne, 'because of the number of French visitors, and also because, unlike some other Europeans, many French people do not speak English. There are also increasing numbers of Japanese and other Far Eastern visitors. Other parts of the job include helping at foreign trade stands promoting the town abroad, and also some translation work for the local authority.

Suzanne sells an item to a foreign visitor. Often, even once the language problem is overcome, visitors have problems handling our currency and make their first attempts in the TIC.

A colleague takes an incoming call. All the staff need to be ready to speak to personal or telephone callers in any of their languages at any time.

other transport matters, right through to queries which may seem minor or even funny but are important to the person concerned.

Suzanne Mantell is deputy manager and senior tourist information officer in a large TIC. 'Mine is often the first face a visitor will see,' says Suzanne, 'so I'm representing my town.' The majority of enquiries come from people who speak good English

and postal enquiries – again, sometimes in foreign languages. Most postal enquiries are simply asking for the type of information which can be given in a brochure but her written languages must be good enough to answer specific queries if necessary. She also updates the many local fact sheets, orders additional copies of leaflets, brochures and goods for sale and keeps the public section of the office tidy and well stocked.

'Working here, I feel as though I've got my finger on the pulse,' says Suzanne. 'I can change people's attitudes. If people have a negative view of the town and perhaps have a complaint which I handle the right way, I can turn that person around and they'll have a nice time here.'

All in a day's work

'We work normal office hours but we extend the opening hours in the summer,' says Suzanne. 'We're open weekends throughout the year and Saturday

enquiries are entered onto the system, then later in the morning we can run off labels and fill envelopes with the relevant information.' The counter and

of the town?". We also have a lot of foreign students who come to Britain to study at one of the two universities in the town. They may be looking for long-term accommodation.' The office only deals with holiday accommodation. 'We have a list of accommodation agencies in the town,' says Suzanne. 'It is rare that we turn anyone away without suggesting where they might find help.'

Language students sometimes come in looking for help with their project work. 'They sometimes ask us how many buttons there are on a policeman's jacket. We can't answer that one!' laughs Suzanne. But she does need to know the town and local area very well. 'To do this job you need a good broad knowledge of the rest of the UK as well,' she adds.

The TIC can become very busy, particularly on Saturdays during the summer months. Some of the enquiries are straightforward and can be quickly dealt with, others take time to research.

is our busiest day, so we work a shift system of five days on and two days off.' Before she opens the office to the public each morning, Suzanne restocks the shelves with free literature and saleable books and maps, gets the till ready and switches the telephone over from its night message service. Then it's time to open the door to the customers.

'The mornings are quietest,' says Suzanne, 'so the first part of the morning is usually spent dealing with postal as well as personal and telephone enquiries. We're fully computerized, so postal and accommodation

telephone, meanwhile, are getting busier all the time. 'Lunchtimes are always busy,' Suzanne continues, 'so lunches are taken on a shift system to keep the office open.'

A stream of visitors

People come into the TIO all the time, some just browse and others wait their turn to ask questions. A German man asks a member of staff for help to sort out a problem with his bank. He speaks no English so the TIO telephones the bank for him. 'The type of enquiry can range from the complicated like that, to "have you got a map

Back-room duties

After lunch Suzanne starts to update a local information sheet. She telephones the organizations listed on the sheet to ensure the details are still correct, looks in the office file for any new leaflets that have been received, then checks local directories and the telephone book for new organizations. This gives her a break from the counter: 'When we're busy in the summer it is non-stop, so we work two hours on the counter then one hour off,' she explains. She also answers some telephone calls: 'It's different using languages face to face, when you have facial expressions to help,' explains Suzanne. 'On the telephone you need a better command of the language.'

Home time

At the end of the day Suzanne cashes up, switches the telephones over and collates the statistics for the day, week or month. 'We keep records of each type of enquiry. We note each one at the counter, on the telephone and by post.' There is also a sensor to count the number of people who walk through the door. The information is used to help review and plan the service.

It's a fact

TICs are operated by local authorities but those in England are part of the English Tourist Board, which is responsible for promoting England within Great Britain. There are separate organizations for Scotland, Wales and Northern Ireland.

The Tourist Board produces a huge amount of literature promoting all different parts of the country. The covers of these brochures reflect the atmospheres of the areas – busy bustling Brighton contrasts with the tranquil New Forest.

Activity

Set up your own tourist information office

You will need:
A counter top
promotional material - collect from a resort or make your own items for 'sale'
a real or mock-up telephone line
tourist information officers; members of the public

Procedure
1. Work out the sort of questions that might be asked. Role-play these questions and find out how it feels to give out information.
2. Record the type of questions you are asked on a form.
3. Have a 'difficult' customer. How easy is it to deal with this sort of person? Can you change their attitude?
4. Have a 'silly' question. Can you keep a straight face and answer it sensibly and helpfully?
5. Try asking the same questions in a foreign language, and see how well you can answer them. Then try it on the telephone (if you can't use a real telephone try speaking with your backs to each other).
6. Collate the data from the record form. Can you see how your service might be improved based on the type of customers you have been helping?

How to become a tourist information officer

Suzanne speaks with a salesman. He is taking an order for books for the shop. This is all part of Suzanne's management work.

'When I was at school I made up my mind that I wanted to use languages. I realized that I had a flair for them. After 'A' levels I decided not to go to university because it would not train me for a specific career, and chose instead to do a bilingual secretarial course.' The course concentrated on French and included a placement in France. Suzanne also speaks German and had done a school exchange to Germany.

At the end of the course Suzanne did temporary work for a while. 'I enjoyed using my languages but didn't like the work very much,' she says. 'Then this job came up.'

There aren't any specific qualifications needed to work as a TIO, although many people are well qualified. The important thing is to be fluent in at least one foreign language, and to demonstrate this with a spoken test at interview. 'After a minimum of six months working as a TIO you can ask to be put forward for an internal qualification at NVQ level 3,' explains Suzanne. Her employer, the local authority, encourages staff into further training: 'I didn't speak Spanish until I began working here, when I learnt it at night school and on an intensive course. There are also learning tapes and videos available and other help towards study.'

Is this the career for you?

'It doesn't take very long to learn about the main places of interest,' advises Suzanne. "You could do that in a weekend. It's more important to have a good sense of humour and enjoy working with people – it can be very, very demanding.'

Although there's a structure to the day, and also to the year, with Bank Holidays and events such as annual festivals, every working day is different. 'You need common-sense and patience,' continues Suzanne. You also need to be polite at all times, even when it's difficult to keep a straight face: 'We have a file of silly questions we have been asked. These include:

- Where can I find a massage machine for my greyhound?
- Are there many fish in the sea?
- Are the banks open in Greece?
- Do you have any photos of the nudist beach?
- Where can I get a portable wheat grinder?
- How will I know when I get to the nudist beach?

These were all serious questions which Suzanne and her colleagues answered as best they could (and yes, they did find a massage machine for the greyhound).

'If you don't like the public you can't give your best – it's very important that you do like working with the public. When it's busy with people are queuing at the door, others trying to buy things and the telephone ringing non-stop, you have to stay calm and be patient. It can be very tiring. But this can be balanced by one nice

Many of Suzanne's customers are language students. They often ask for details of tourist outings. Although they come to learn English, at the start of their stay many of them need Suzanne and her colleagues to speak to them in their native tongue.

customer, who can turn our day around in the same way we try to turn theirs around.'

'With languages you need to be conversationally fluent: it's not enough to be able to direct people around the town. You may have to discuss transferring their flights or something technical. Although you don't need the actual qualification you probably need degree-level in a second language, as well as the confidence to use it.'

Career planning

Contact your local tourist information office and ask whether an officer can come to your school or college to talk about the work. Ask them about the best and worst parts of the job.

Making Career Connections

Send for prospectuses for any likely looking courses.

Write to a conference town's marketing department and ask for their foreign marketing material. Explain why you want it and ask for any careers information they hold.

Look into courses to help improve your languages and give you customer contact. Speak to your careers adviser about this.

Getting started

Interested in being a tourist information officer? Here's what you can do now.

1. Join a language circle to improve your foreign language.
2. Overcome any shyness about using your languages. Become bold and confident.
3. Gain some experience in a customer care role, such as a Saturday job in a shop or waiting in a restaurant.

Related careers

Bureau de change cashier
Deals in foreign currency, changing it into sterling and back. May deal with British tourists before they travel or foreign visitors to the UK.

Conference sales officer
Promotes a town or city as a venue for conferences. Brings in foreign customers. Languages are often only a small part of this role.

Tourist guide
Takes parties of foreign visitors on walking or coach tours. May need to be multi-lingual.

Tour company worker
Puts together holiday package tours. Liaises with foreign resorts by letter, telephone or in person. May negotiate contracts with hotels or car hire firms.

Future watch

This job is going to become more and more computerized, with more touch-screen computers and Internet access for both customers and officers. 'But there will always be a place for speaking face to face with customers,' says Suzanne. 'Leisure time generally has increased, and people are travelling again now that they have money. Leisure and tourism is a growth industry.'

It's a fact

Suzanne's office handles more than 300,000 queries a year – well over one for each person who lives in the town (about 250,000 people).

Much of the data Suzanne uses is at hand through the computer system.

David Grace

European Officer

PERSONAL PROFILE

Career: European officer. 'I find out what's going on in the European Union – new policies, new laws, new money for projects – and I advise the council on which bits matter to them.'

Interests: Travelling, politics, philosophy, history. 'I'm also interested in artificial intelligence and computers. I listen to music a lot; I particularly like electric folk music.'

Latest accomplishment: 'It's often not the external accomplishments that count but aspects such as getting the resources to do the job. When I came, I was on my own and now I have a team of five people.'

Why I do what I do: 'I'm fascinated by the development of the European Union and I like widening the horizons of local government.'

I am: 'Very sociable and extrovert. I prefer taking on new challenges to doing the same old thing. I get bored by routine. I like to plan things in great detail to be sure they work. I like setting things up and handing them over to other people to keep them going. And I hope I am persuasive.'

What I wanted to be when I was at school: A politician.

What a European officer does

When people talk about 'European money', what do they actually mean? It's all to do with the European Union (EU). The United Kingdom is a member of the European Union, an organization formed in 1957 with an initial six member states. There are now 15 members, with more due to join before 2010. It was originally inspired by the desire to create a lasting peace in Europe after the two world wars, and now employs many thousands of people in Brussels and Strasbourg.

David refers to his map of Europe. The bottle was a gift from a group of visiting Europeans.

One of the main roles of the EU is to encourage member countries to develop economically – to become richer, more productive, and more efficient in what they do. This benefits each country individually as well as the EU, and so Europe becomes stronger in the world marketplace. Part of the way the EU helps member states is to give money for projects, some of which are huge and others tiny. David Grace works for a county council as its European officer and his job is to make the most of the EU to benefit the county. 'The funds bit is what attracts everyone's attention,' explains David, 'and is 80 per cent of the work, if not more. Anyone doing this job has to know about European funding, but I hope the job is more than that – I try to make it more than that.' Funding can be to help redevelop a region which has lost its old industries, for instance, or can be used to help unemployed people gain new skills through training and work experience.

'European work is not a luxury,' insists David. 'It's another dimension to the ordinary work of the council. The slogan on our strategy document is "Wider horizons for stronger services" and

David checks details with other members of the Europe office. He works with a team of five staff, recruited since he took over as European officer two years ago. They each have their own responsibilities and help to provide European information, training and support to a wide range of organizations in the county.

it sums up our integrated approach. We have to work with central government and Brussels is now part of the picture, but a lot of people would like to ignore that fact. We're a county council and we have got to live in the real world.'

Pleased when people stop coming

One local European-funded project is a day centre where disabled people came in to do 'not very interesting work'. With European funding it was totally revamped. The person running the centre knew it had been successful when people stopped coming – they were getting jobs with the new skills they had learned at the centre. This is one of the aims of the European Social Fund – to spend money employing people to give them skills.

This is the European flag. The circle of stars represents the union of the people of Europe. There are always twelve stars, representing perfection and entirety. There is also a European anthem that has been adapted from the final movement of Beethoven's 9th Symphony.

All in a day's work

David is based in the county council's offices where he spends about three days a week. He visits Brussels on average three days a month, and has other meetings across the county and country. 'Every day in the office I check through the post and messages to see if there's anything urgent,' says David. Some of these messages are in French. 'I read and write letters and can hold telephone conversations in French,' he continues. 'Telephone calls are one of the most difficult things because we are used to talking to people face to face, reading their lips and watching their facial expressions. On the telephone the non-verbal clues aren't there.' He also knows basic German and Italian. 'French is the main language. The Germans speak very good English. I think German will become more important though, when the Eastern European states join the EU in 2000.' It is not just the

David plugs his laptop computer in to the mains and telephone points wherever he can, and when he is travelling it can work for a limited time on battery-power.

language that can make communication difficult: 'Other nationalities have different ways of running meetings,' David explains. 'There are lots of cultural differences I need to be aware of.'

Many aspects to one job

David explains what his job entails: 'The first thing is to make sure we have all the information we need,' says David. 'We gather information about the policies of the EU that might affect our

work, how the work might change, the timetable, what funds are available and when, the application conditions and so on. To gather this information, organizations like us have a Brussels office. The office is shared as a lot of our work is in partnership with other organizations. We also look at information put out by the European Commission, and get a lot more from the Internet. A lot of information comes by word of mouth, by networking.'

David explains how there's no point just gathering information: 'We also disseminate information. If there are busy officers running a children's home, for example, they haven't got time to be aware that there might be some funding available. We have to get the information to them, and there are various ways we do this.'

Holding hands

'Most people find form-filling a real hurdle,' explains David. 'We persuade people in the county to think up projects that might gain funding and we help them fill in

The chamber where elected members of the council meet. The flag indicates the council's commitment to Europe.

the forms - we "hold their hands". It's a process of stimulating, encouraging, helping with details and then following through and making sure the application gets to the right bit of the Commission. That's the bulk of the work.

'We also find out what new policies are being developed within the EU and what opportunities there are to influence these to the benefit of the county. This is lobbying at European level: ensuring the people making the decisions are aware of the arguments. The chances that the one officer in the EU who is drafting the legislation knows what is of interest to people in our county is tiny. It's a case of knowing who to talk to, when to talk to them and the limits of their job: it's no good talking to the wrong person.'

Other aspects

'There's a certain amount of formal work, such as when councillors come over from France and I write speeches for the Chairman – he has so many engagements he couldn't possibly write all his own speeches. I do a little bit of interpreting and translating, especially if I'm travelling in France with the elected members, who rarely speak French. As with most jobs, the higher you go more in management, the more administration work there is, some is good and some not. There is a certain amount of financial work, which is not desperately exciting, but the personnel side of it is very good.'

What is a network and what is networking?

These are two similar words with different meanings. A 'network' is a system of computers linked together within an organization. The term 'networking', though, is used to describe people getting together (or using the telephone, post, e-mail or other means of communication) and talking. This is still, in our high-tech information age, one of the main ways of gathering useful information and feedback in many organizations. The ability to network is vital in many jobs.

Activity

Apply for funding
Many jobs involve making formal applications for money. Try doing this yourself, alone or in a group.

You will need:
A project you feel needs extra funding. This could be a real community project you are involved in or a fictional project. You won't be able to make an actual application yourself but you can go through many of the stages to see how it works.
Access to information on funding: your local library and/or a specialist library; access to the Internet; the support of an adult who is knowledgeable about funding. A librarian may be able to help.

Procedure
1. Look at the project and think how it could be improved with additional funds. Think about:
- its goals: will these remain as they are?
- any changes ahead: how could these affect the project?
- its current work and how effective this is.
- improvements that extra funding would make possible.
2. Draw up an action plan. You need to write or draw out the project as it is now and how you hope it will be after receiving funding. You could do this in note form on a computer, or draw large charts. Then note all the changes, why they are necessary and the positive effects they will have.
3. Work out how much all these changes will cost and when you want to make them. Will this be all at once or in stages?
4. Find out about possible funding. Look at EU funding and also at the National Lottery and local sources of cash – fund-raising organizations often give money to local projects. There are other sources of funding too – see how many you can find.
5. Make sure that your project fits the criteria required for obtaining funds, and then make your application. Get it in by the deadline!
6. Do you think your application would be successful? Ask an expert. Perhaps it's worth getting together with a project that needs funds and trying it for real.

How to become a European officer

'This is our accord with the Hungarian county of Veszprim. It describes the areas where we are going to co-operate. It's an expression of goodwill,' says David.

David trained as a lawyer and then ran an international youth organization in Brussels. 'That was when I developed my French,' he explains. 'Then I came back to Britain, and wrote a book. Britain was overstocked with lawyers and there were jobs in computing so I went into the computer industry, designing software. I liked the software design, it was very interesting, but I didn't have a natural flair for it.' After some time in marketing he became demoralized and left. David took a part-time job and stood for parliament, campaigning for a federal Europe. When he didn't win the parliamentary seat he got a job in local government.

Following this David spent another five years in Brussels working in three different roles, before returning to the UK and his current job. 'It's fairly unusual for European Officers to have both European and local government experience, though some have done a year or two in Brussels,' he says.

Is this the career for you?

Not every council has a European officer, but there are increasing numbers in local government as well as in universities, trade federations, regional development agencies and some companies. Even so, competition for this sort of work is intense. 'You need at least one other language, and more is an advantage,' explains David. 'There are lots of people in the world these days who have got two languages, especially in Europe, masses and masses of them. If they want a successful career they need something else, some added value like their knowledge of how European institutions work, for example. When I started doing this work and went to Brussels for the first time, my French was diabolical. I picked up the language doing the work. It was my knowledge of the subject that got me the job'

As well as this you need to be able to relate at all levels: 'You deal with central government civil servants, other local authorities, private sector, voluntary sector and people in Brussels, the Eurocrats.' You need to be persuasive to overcome people's inertia, personable, and enthusiastic. 'You mustn't be shy, you've got to go out and meet people and persuade them to do things. You've got to be able to negotiate. You need an interest in the way other cultures work. It's important that you're thorough and give attention to detail. You've got to be able to work on your own, as some EOs

Although David's role is centred on Europe he is often called upon to host visits from people from all over the world, not just Europe. Here he is with visiting Japanese students.

don't have a team, and you have to be a self-starter. You've got to be flexible and willing to travel.'

Working in local government is more risky than it used to be, explains David: 'A new council could close this office. It's a fact of life. You've got to look ahead, you can't wait for things to go wrong.' He has to tell his employers what he is doing and how well it is going. 'You've got to constantly tell them: Look, we've just achieved this. It's a form of selling, but selling ideas.' Because of the risky nature of this work, David advises getting a qualification first. 'It's never a bad idea to have a professional qualification,' he says. 'You can always fall back on professional work.'

Career planning

Ask your careers adviser about the 'stagiaire' scheme, which enables new graduates to gain several months' experience in Brussels. Decide how you can gain enough experience now to enable you to apply successfully for a 'stage' later on. Make and keep contacts who could help you with this.

Making Career Connections

Contact or visit the European Commission London office and collect written information about the EU, its institutions and workings and career openings. Find the address at your careers office or on the EU web site (see below).

Look in your careers library for information about careers in Europe. Write to the appropriate office and ask for further information. Research degree courses in European studies.

Contact your local authority's Europe Office and ask if you can spend some time work-shadowing or on work experience.

Getting started

Interested in being a European Officer? Here's what you can do now.

1. Keep working at your languages. Make sure you go on foreign exchanges, and work abroad if possible.
2. Find a foreign penpal: look at sites that interest you on the Internet and see whether anyone with similar interests would like to correspond via e-mail or post.
3. Research the EU and its institutions. Use your library (many have European Information Relay Points) or visit the web site at *http://www.europa.eu.int* Even showing a little knowledge of the institutions will put you ahead.
4. For more information, or to gain an idea of the scale of the EU, ask to visit a European Documentation Centre. These are often housed in universities. They hold every single official document produced by the EU. Find your nearest one via the EU web site of the EU London office.
5. Contact your local MEP (Member of the European Parliament) and ask for an interview for your school newspaper.

Related careers

Here are some related careers you may want to look into.

Librarian
Chooses, organizes and promotes the use of materials such as books and magazines for clients. Assists users with enquiries. May work in general public libraries, academic or specialist libraries.

Fundraiser
Obtains as much money as possible from a diverse range of sources such as the National Lottery. Researches, applies, and follows through applications. May work for a charity or other organization.

Economic development officer
Works in local government to attract inward investment. Supports small- and medium-sized businesses with advice and information. May overlap with the work of the European officer.

Regional development agency officer
Will work to promote investment and economic growth in local agency area once the agencies have been set up, probably by the end of 1998.

Future watch

There will be less EU funds coming to Britain from the year 2000, once the Eastern European countries have joined. 'Some local authorities will give up,' says David, 'but the sensible ones will need good European Officers. The EU is developing a responsibility for employment – there will be European funds directed at improving employability, and possibly creating employment. Economic and monetary union will happen and Britain will join, I think, so the role of the European Officer will change, but the continued economic integration of Britain into the EU means there will continue to be a demand for European Officers.'

Cherry Clarke – Research Assistant

There are plenty of back-room workers behind any public organization, and the European Union is no exception. Cherry Clarke works as a self-employed research assistant for three Members of the European Parliament (MEPs). Her job is varied: 'I look after the UK office for one of the MEPs,' says Cherry. 'I am his constituency person and I deal with the initial sifting of enquiries, all his travel arrangements and the day-to-day running of the office.' Although she is based in the UK she travels to Strasbourg, where Parliament is in session, one week each month, and Brussels, where the administrative centre is based, probably 12 times a year. 'I go out when I feel I need to,' explains Cherry. 'With new technology I can pick up everything I need on the Internet and various systems, but I find one of the most useful aspects of these trips is to keep my contacts going.'

Using contacts

Cherry has been in this kind of work for nearly 20 years and has 'built up a wealth of contacts and knowledge.' 'I know who to approach,' she says. She may be asked to investigate matters such as trying to find European funding for a certain project for a constituent. She needs to know who to contact and where to find information. 'Even if I feel there's nothing I can do to assist them, I still try,' she says. Another key part of the job is escorting constituency groups to Brussels and Strasbourg. 'We normally find that after three or four days even the most Euro-sceptical are converted!'

Cherry (right) is based in the constituency office of one of the MEPs she works for. She handles day-to-day queries and problems, and liaises with members of the constituency office staff.

Community languages

There are many official languages in the European Union and each is simultaneously interpreted to MEPs and delegates during sessions. This process has sometimes been criticized as a waste of resources in an organization where so many people are multilingual, but as Cherry explains: 'We can't afford to have misunderstandings over technical jargon. It's important that each speaker is absolutely certain that others have understood what he or she has said.'

Cherry uses her languages less now than when she first started the work. 'The Community has increased in size and the new countries tend to speak English,' explains Cherry. But even if the person she needs to call speaks English well, first she needs to get through to them, and that could mean using any of her additional languages: French, Spanish and Italian. She also needs plenty of other skills and qualities: 'You must be outgoing and patient,' she says.

'Also very good on the telephone and very organized – you need to keep track of what you're doing and not lose sight of projects. You really do have to be interested in Europe, to like people and have plenty of initiative.' You also need to develop good research and writing skills and have plenty of common sense. 'You have to be adaptable and take anything that's thrown at you,' adds Cherry. 'It's very varied and, like every job, it's what you make of it.'

Cherry reports how we tend to see the European Union, via the media, with a cynical eye. 'In the UK there's still a "fog in the Channel cut-off" attitude,' she says, then adds: 'Westminster can appear grey and dowdy and stuck in a time warp but in Strasbourg there's an energy – this is where the future is.'

Getting started

1. Go to your reference library and read directories on the history and workings of the European Community. Find details of associated lobbying and trade organizations, all of which employ linguists.
2. Contact your local MEP's office. Ask if you can help with clerical work. Watch and listen to what goes on.
3. Develop a general interest in world, European and domestic affairs. Read more than one newspaper to get a broad view.
4. Talk to people you know who are in work. You may find they have connections with Europe. Ask them about it.

Jeremy Davies – Technical Writer

Jeremy Davies works as a technical writer for a large engineering company in Sweden. His department produces operation and maintenance documentation to accompany each of their new trains delivered to any country in the world. This may mean writing the documentation in English, or having it translated into the appropriate language. He speaks fluent Swedish, learnt since he moved to

Jeremy writes at his computer and stays in touch with offices and clients throughout the world via e-mail.

Jeremy in front of the new Stockholm metro car – one of a wide range of products produced by Adtranz.

the country eight years ago, and uses this in conversations and meetings at work. 'I tend to write everything in English,' says Jeremy, 'memos, e-mails and so on. Also, I tend to be put onto projects delivering trains to English-speaking countries so I can use my English to best effect.'

Jeremy's bilingual skills are useful throughout the company: 'I get people from the marketing department who are producing brochures in English come to me and say "please can you proof-read this?". Although Swedes are generally very good at English, it's never one hundred per cent correct.'

Language

If a customer is happy for their staff to work from English manuals then the documentation will be delivered in English. There are exceptions, however. 'Documentation related to safety or maintenance may have to be in that country's mother tongue – their safety agency can insist on it,' explains Jeremy. His department does not have staff covering every possible language. 'We may send material to a translation service. It can be very difficult, for example, to find translators working from Swedish to Turkish. We may have to translate into English first. And then once it's been translated into Turkish, we have to ensure that it is correct.'

Losing touch with English

Linguists always work translating or interpreting from their second language into their mother tongue. That way the finished translation sounds polished and exactly right.

'For me one of the big problems with living abroad,' says Jeremy, 'is losing my English. If you learn enough of a new language you eventually start thinking in it. Then when you speak English you sound like a foreigner speaking English – not the accent but the grammar and sentence structure. For someone living abroad and earning a living based on translation it can be a major problem.'

Jeremy really enjoys speaking two languages. 'Swedes always come and ask things about language – it leads to interesting discussions about things I've never considered before. I'd thoroughly recommend moving to a new country and learning a new language and a new culture. It's good, and it's not the big deal some people make it out to be.'

Getting started

1. Contact a large engineering company and ask for information about careers in technical writing.
2. Visit your careers library for information about working abroad. There are no official restrictions on working within the European Community but other countries have their own criteria for work permits.
3. Ask your careers adviser for details of degree courses which include a year abroad. Send for prospectuses and find out where you might go and what sort of work you would do there.
4. Consider a gap year working abroad to see how you adapt to a new culture. The experience will greatly benefit your knowledge of the language even if you decide that you prefer living in the UK.

Francine Mortimer – Translator

Francine at work in her home office. As well as translating, she also tutors young people in languages and runs a translation agency. She needs the latest technology to be able to present her work professionally and send it electronically if necessary.

Where do you go if you receive a letter in Russian that you don't understand? This happens frequently in business. It could be any type of document in any language. Some organizations have translators working inhouse

but many organizations, as well as private individuals, turn to freelance translators like Francine Mortimer for help.

World-wide translation

Francine explains what she does: 'Once I receive work I read through it quickly first,' she says, 'to understand the gist of it. I make sure I have the right dictionaries, then start going through the text.' If Francine isn't a specialist in the area she's translating, she will ask the client for background information. 'A proper translator would not return more than two to three thousand words a day back to the client,' she explains. 'You have to allow

almost as much time for checking the translating, as you do for the actual translating. A spell-checker in the relevant language is essential. New technology has made this job easier: 'There's a translators' forum on the Internet,' Francine says. She explains how easy it is to use but adds that the process takes time: 'You have to allow enough time for an answer to come back.

Working freelance

Francine enjoys the freedom of working from home but points out that there are drawbacks: 'You have to be happy to be alone. You've got to be on top of current computing developments too.

'If you like words and learning generally, you will learn a lot from translating: about the subject matter or the way the language is changing. You also have to be meticulous.'

Offering something different

Francine has careers advice to offer: 'Don't just do languages, do something else as well. The people who do well out of translating are those with languages that are unusual, but are sufficiently

widespread. It's very hard to get your foot in the door with French and German. Ideally you need the experience of jobs and industry. You might get a job as a new graduate inside a translating agency. I would consider getting a job that uses languages first, to get this specialist knowledge. And you've got to be fairly bright – clients expect you to be perfect even when the text they give you is very badly written.'

How did Francine find her original contacts? 'I got the Paris Yellow Pages and wrote to a number of companies,' says Francine. 'It is also a good idea to look for work through agencies as they have contacts abroad.'

Getting started

1. Think about a specialist subject apart from languages and investigate this as a career option?
2. Buy or borrow a foreign language CD-Rom to improve your fluency.
3. Translate an article, with help from your teacher. If it's an historical document that has no copyright, you can try to get it published.
4. Buy a suitable magazine when abroad and subscribe to it from home.
5. Watch simple programmes on satellite TV in the relevant languages.

Ben Ashcroft – Publishing Sales Representative

Ben's essential sales kit – a folder and small display stand containing information on the books his company is going to bring out in the next six months.

We all visit bookshops, either to browse or to look for specific titles – but how do booksellers know which books we are likely to want? Ben Ashcroft is a publishing 'rep'. 'I work for a big academic publisher,' says Ben. 'Once a book has been produced it's handed to the marketing and sales departments. The marketing department tells the people who might buy the book that it exists, and the sales reps go to the customers and encourage them to buy it.'

Chatting in German

'We sell most of our books through bookshops,' explains Ben. 'A sales rep tells people about the books and takes orders, and also persuades them to promote the books for us through their own catalogues or shop displays.' Ben's customers are all overseas. 'The European market for books in English is quite big, because most people educated to university level in Europe can read English.' Ben's employer, Cambridge University Press, has reps working worldwide, and Ben sells their books in Austria and Germany. Although many of his customers speak good English, Ben's conversations are in German. 'I speak German to them because it's easier for them and they'll be more relaxed,' he explains. 'It's a two-way process. I listen to what they're saying to me, find out what our competitors are doing and get ideas for new books.'

The sales process

'I travel for two or three weeks at a time. I have about 650 customers in Germany and visit five or six a day. We sit down and talk about books. My company produces 1500 new books each year, and one of the problems with working for such a big company is getting my mind around every series of books – I have to know the lists.'

Ben continues, 'I suggest things they might want to buy, and they say no or yes, and give me an order. The skill of the job is knowing which books will sell to which people. It's not hard selling, but more about: "What do you think of that? This would be a good idea." I listen to their opinions. I also make sure the bookseller has stocks of the older books.'

Back home

Ben also spends time in the UK. 'When I have spoken to customers, there are always matters to follow up and promotions to organize. I spend a great deal of time on the phone or faxing and e-mailing customers. There's also a lot of feedback going backwards and forwards, with my boss, the editors and marketing people.'

Although his job is demanding, Ben enjoys it. 'It's fun, as long as you can cope with your life being disrupted and being very busy all the time. My territory is my responsibility – there is a great deal of freedom. It's never boring, and I'm working with a nice product – everyone is interested in books.'

Getting started

1. Go into bookshops and identify the different publishers who produced the books. See how many types of publisher you can find.
2. How good are you at persuading people to do things? in a group, pull random items from a bag and take turns 'selling' these to each other.
3. 'Employers want skills other than just one language,' says Ben. Investigate degree courses that include other aspects as well as your favourite languages.
4. When you've read a book, think about how you would present it in a catalogue and how you would sell it. Consider how you would do this in another language.

Classified Advertising

HELP WANTED

EXPANDING BUSINESS NEEDS PARTNERS
Full and part time. You are: ambitious, open-minded determined to SUCCEED. *No capital requirement.* Send CV to: Jan Smith, 62 Albert Street, Bigley-by-Sea, BG9 7NT

CANTONESE/ENGLISH BILINGUAL ACCOUNT EXECUTIVE
LEADING telecommunications company is currently expanding in the Oriental communities. Candidate should have at least 2 years' sales and marketing experience, insurance experie... are an asset. £20... + QUALIFIED applicant... Please contact Pe... Manager, NCM Con... East Bigley R... Plumchester, PH9 ...

SUB-EDITOR wa...
women's mag... writing exper... essential. Pl... Nancy Lan... Nightingale ...uild... Church Stre... H9 5...

Pharmaceut...

GRAPHIC ...TIST
Our busy A...ising De... and lay out ...rs, print a...
Your rela... college ... experience th...cludes fa... and QuarkXP... You wo... priorities and ...work to ...
Please forwa... ...ur CV to ... Trade, Summer... errace, ... 555 4112. We a... ...equal op...

ACTING INSTRUCT...
Olivier College requires ...ing Instructor for the au... winter academic year. This ... half-time position for a ten-month contract beginning mid August.
The Instructor will teach both Introductory and Intermediate Acting for 1st and 2nd year students. Possible opportunities to direct College productions exist but is not a job requirement.
Previous teaching experience essential. Bachelor's degree, ·acting and directing experience required. Master's degree in a related field preferred.
Deadline for application is 25 June. Enquiries can be directed to the Personnel Department or send a CV and covering letter.
Olivier College
45 Lawrence Street
East Plumchester PH12 7FX

CITY DISPATCHER WANTED
Busy City dispatch requires innovative person to run local truck operation. Require good knowledge of ocean cargo. Apply in confidence to: GENERAL MANAGER PO Box 4329, New Amsterdam, Plumchester, PH6 2NF

SALES REPRESENTATIVE

DUTIES:
Promote a... ...d quality window... ... products to the ...uilding market in the city.
QUALIFICATIONS:
- Minimum three years' sale... perience in related ...
- An ...

... will ...anical ap-... sset. Good command ...nglish necessary. Call ABC ... ...55 6391 for more information.
Please telephone between 9 am and 12 noon Monday to Thursday only.

FIRSTLINE HEALTH & FITNESS CLUB
Firstline Health & Fitness Clubs, expanding through Plumchester and the surrounding area, offers an exciting and rewarding career in the health & fitness industry. We are currently searching for sales individuals with strong interpersonal skills in the following positions.

1. Membership Consultant
2. Corporate Sales — must have corporate sales experience
3. Programme Consultant
4. Cardio Tester

Qualifications:
- Minimum 2 years' direct sales experience
- Background in aerobic & anaerobic training
- Knowledge of nutrition

Qualified applicants are invited to call Steve Florry for an information pack 555 1305 or fax your CV to 555 1304.

SCARBIN AND BOXWELL GENERAL HOSPITAL

Registered Nurses
In-patient Services
• Full and Part-time
An active acute care facility, the new In-patient Mental Health Department, will provide the experienced mental healthcare professional or professionals motivated to pursue career in mental health nursing with an ideal opportunity to broaden their group, interviewing, and counselling skills in a supportive and cooperative setting. The background of the ideal candidate will include recent experience in primary nursing care. General qualifications include a Certificate of Competence from the Royal College of Psychiatric ...

...reation Therapist
...n consultation ... ...ary nurses, you will ...es an... ...ivities of all types ...do asses... ...patient leisure ...izations a... ...lanning com- ...ptions are ...able. As the ...e year of e... ...ence in an ...g a recogniz... ...recreation ...
... and Boxwe... ...eneral ...onals dedicat... ...their ...are invited to ...ly in ...well General H...tal,

...anage...
...age Carpente... ...age ... ...e carpe... ...y and ...ition, ...didates ...perso... ...elected ...epo... ...rectly to ... ...the various ...Philharmonic ...nefit programme. ...oduction Manager, ...rts, teleph... ...555 7474 ... ...your CV and hand... ...en letter to: **Cheryl Wade,** ...ngton Centre for Perfo... ...g Arts, Vaudeville Road, ...nchester, PH1 6FT.

Start Your Own O... Cleaning R...
Be ...., part time in ...ng, cleaning shops and offices.
For more information call 555 5190

Weller

JOURNEYMAN MACHINIST
General Machinist, preferably with milling experience required for precision machine shop manufacturing electromechanical sensors. Minimum 5-10 years' related experience. Must be capable of reading detailed drawings and working to extremely close tolerances.
No telephone calls please. Forward CVs to:

Mrs P Weller
Fred Weller Corporation
34 Leslie Road
Plumchester PH8 0BT

AWARDS FOR BUSINESS EXCELLENCE

Bilingual Customer Services Trainee

Plumchester Card Services is keen to recruit a trainee in our customer services department. The role involves telephoning and receiving calls from business customers and potential customers and explaining the benefits of our financial services. We have a large French customer base through our overseas offices and applicants should be fluent French speakers. Some knowledge of written French is also required.

Other requirements include good interpersonal skills, an easy manner on the telephone and willingness to learn.

If you are interested in this exciting and challenging role in a young and expanding company please telephone Mrs Carol Caldwell on 5554799 for more information.

Who got the job?

Finding a job

The first step to success in any career is finding a job. But how do you go about finding one?

- Talk to family, friends and neighbours and let them know what jobs interest you.
- Respond to 'Help Wanted' ads in newspapers.

- Pin an advertisement of your skills on a community notice board.

- Register at Government and private employment agencies.

- Contact potential employers by phone or in person.
- Send out speculative letters and follow up with phone calls.

A job application usually consists of a letter and a curriculum vitae (CV – a summary of your experience and qualifications for the job). Applicants whose CVs show they are qualified may be invited to a job interview.

Activity

Recruiting a bilingual trainee

The advertisement on the opposite page invites applications for a trainee's job in a well-known successful financial services company. The job is to tell people about the credit card services on offer and persuade them to apply for a card – it is a sales job. Jobs like this demand very good person-to-person skills and a commitment to learning fast and succeeding in a competitive environment. There are often jobs like this advertised because a lot of people find they don't get on with selling or the lively atmosphere, but for the right person it is an excellent starting point for many people-related careers.

Applicants are asked to telephone Mrs Caldwell. This is in reality the first job interview: for a job using the telephone it is an easy way to see whether the applicants come across well on the phone. Mrs Caldwell will make notes about this conversation and then wait for letters and CVs before deciding which applicants to interview face-to-face.

Two of the applicants were Julia McClung and Jeff Ali. The notes Mrs Caldwell made during the phone conversation and their letters and CVs are shown on pages 46 and 47.

Procedure

Make a list of the qualities that you think are important for a good bilingual sales trainee in a financial services company. Now consider each applicant's CV, covering letter and performance on the phone. Which candidate has the best qualifications and experience? Would you invite them back for a second interview? What else would you like to find out about them?

Challenge

How would you perform at a job interview? Role-play an interview in which a friend plays the part of Mrs Caldwell, then reverse the roles. Do this face-to-face and by pretending to be on the phone. This practice can help make sure that when you apply for a job, you have a good chance of getting it!

Julia McClung's application and interview

144 Manor Green Road
Wimborne Green
Nr Plumchester
PL5 7CN

22 June 19-

Mrs Carol Caldwell
Human Resources Manager
Plumchester Card Services
West Green
Plumchester PH21 2LS

Dear Mrs Caldwell

Thank you for explaining the customer services trainee job to me on the telephone this morning. I found everything you said very interesting – and I had no idea all this went on in Plumchester!

I enclose my CV as you suggested. You will see that I am very active socially and enjoy persuading people to do things, whether it's to go bowling or to lend me a fiver! I have also done a lot of shop work which involved selling things to people, which I did very well.

I want to continue this work and get more experience, as well as have some real training. I hope you find my CV interesting and I look forward to meeting you at interview.

Yours sincerely

Julia McClung

Telephone interview: Julia McClung

* Spoke clearly and smiled down the line.

* Had not researched the company or job at all.

* Spoke almost perfect French.

* Was polite and did not falter with difficult questions.

* Admitted if she didn't know something, agreed to call back with a reply.

* Keen to have a job.

* Very attractive personality but perhaps a little too ebullient?

Curriculum Vitae

Name: Julia McClung
Address: 144 Manor Green Road
Wimborne Green
Nr Plumchester
PL5 7CN
Date of birth: 8 August 19-

Education
I was at school in both Britain and France. I studied for three years in a primary school just outside Paris when I was aged 7–10. Then I came back to the UK and finished my education here with A levels in French and English. I kept my French language going with frequent visits to family in France.

Work Experience
Plumchester Newsagents: Saturday and holiday work for the last four years
Market stall, Paris: selling my home-made goods occasionally in a craft market
Guest House: entertaining and waiting on guests at my parents' small hotel

Interests
I like all types of socializing and getting to know all sorts of people. I also like music and fashion, and enjoy shopping.
References: Available on request

22 June 19-

79 Manor Road
Plumchester
PH3 6KA

Mrs Carol Caldwell
Human Resources Manager
Plumchester Card Services
West Green
Plumchester PH21 2LS

Dear Mrs Caldwell

Re: Bilingual customer services trainee

Further to this morning's telephone conversation I have pleasure in enclosing my curriculum vitae.
I have spent much time in France over the last four years and would like to use my language in my work. The sort of role you were describing sounds just right as an introduction and training ground for my career. I would ideally like to work in international management.
I have just finished my A level courses and hope that I may be able to work for your company. I look forward to hearing from you.

Yours sincerely

Jeff Ali

Curriculum Vitae

Jeff Ali
79 Manor Road
Plumchester
PH3 6KA

I am a dedicated and hard-working student and have used the last few years to gain experience of work while studying for my exams. My employers have said that they are impressed with my work and are willing to supply good references. I am looking for a career in an international company where I can use my languages to the benefit of my employer.

Education
Plumchester Sixth Form College
A levels in English, French, German, results due in August
10 GCSEs grades A–C
School exchanges for the last four years, two to France and two to Germany.

Work experience
Plumchester Marina: collecting berthing fees; discussing repairs with owners from all over Europe; advising on all local matters.
Little Plum Language School: assisting with the administration and registration of young students from all over the world.
Plumchester Garage: Selling petrol.

Interests
Reading, local history, debating, European culture, management issues, driving, listening to music.
References; Available on request

**Telephone interview:
Jeff Ali**

* Had a lovely mellow voice, very easy to listen to.

* Knew all about the company and the type of work we do.

* Understood that this is a sales job and what that means, but does he really want to sell?

* Slightly faltering at times.

* Perhaps a little serious? Might not fit into the lively team atmosphere.

* Had very good 'school French' but perhaps not fluent enough for the job?

Index

Credits

(l=left; r = right; t = top;
  b = bottom; c = centre;
  bl = bottom left;
  br = bottom right)

All photographs by Joanna
  Grigg, except Page 6(l): Mo
  Fini, Tumi Collection
Page 7(br): Tumi Music
Page 8: Mo Fini, Tumi
  Collection

Page 13: Birmingham City
  Council, Social Services
  Department
Page 17(b): Miles Cowsill/ Stena
  Line
Page 23(t): American Express
Page 24(t): American Express
Page 31: English Tourist Board
Page 32(c): EF International
  Language Schools
Page 35(r): ECSC - EC - EAEC,
  Brussels-Luxembourg, 1995,
  1996, 1997
Page 41 (c) : Adtranz